William Shakespeare's

The Merchant of Venice

Text by
Garrett T. Caples
Instructor of English
University of California at Berkeley,
Berkeley, California

Illustrations by
Karen Pica

Research & Education Association

MAXnotes™ for
THE MERCHANT OF VENICE

Printed in the United States of America

Library of Congress Catalog Card Number 95-071264

International Standard Book Number 0-87891-026-3

MAXnotes™ is a trademark of
Research & Education Association, Piscataway, New Jersey 08854

What **MAXnotes**™ *Will Do for You*

This book is intended to help you absorb the essential contents and features of William Shakespeare's *The Merchant of Venice* and to help you gain a thorough understanding of the work. The book has been designed to do this more quickly and effectively than any other study guide.

For best results, this **MAXnotes** book should be used as a companion to the actual work, not instead of it. The interaction between the two will greatly benefit you.

To help you in your studies, this book presents the most up-to-date interpretations of every section of the actual work, followed by questions and fully explained answers that will enable you to analyze the material critically. The questions also will help you test your understanding of the work and will prepare you for discussions and exams.

Meaningful illustrations are included to further enhance your understanding and enjoyment of the literary work. The illustrations are designed to place you into the mood and spirit of the work's settings.

The **MAXnotes** also include summaries, character lists, explanations of plot, and section-by-section analyses. A biography of the author and discussion of the work's historical context will help you put this literary piece into the proper perspective of what is taking place.

The use of this study guide will save you the hours of preparation time that would ordinarily be required to arrive at a complete grasp of this work of literature. You will be well prepared for classroom discussions, homework, and exams. The guidelines that are included for writing papers and reports on various topics will prepare you for any added work which may be assigned.

The **MAXnotes** will take your grades "to the max."

Dr. Max Fogiel
Program Director

Contents

**Each scene includes List of Characters,
Summary, Analysis, Study Questions and
Answers, and Suggested Essay Topics.**

Introduction

The Life and Work of William Shakespeare

The details of William Shakespeare's life are sketchy, mostly mere surmise based upon court or other clerical records. His parents, John and Mary (Arden), were married about 1557; she was of the landed gentry, and he was a yeoman—a glover and commodities merchant. By 1568, John had risen through the ranks of town government and held the position of high bailiff, which was a position similar to a mayor. William, the eldest son and the third of eight children, was born in 1564, probably on April 23, several days before his baptism on April 26 in Stratford-upon-Avon. Shakespeare is also believed to have died on the same date-April 23-in 1616.

It is believed that William attended the local grammar school in Stratford where his parents lived, and that he studied primarily Latin, rhetoric, logic, and literature. Shakespeare probably left school at age 15, which was the norm, to take a job, especially since this was the period of his father's financial difficulty. At age 18 (1582), William married Anne Hathaway, a local farmer's daughter who was eight years his senior. Their first daughter (Susanna) was born six months later (1583), and twins Judith and Hamnet were born in 1585.

Shakespeare's life can be divided into three periods: the first 20 years in Stratford, which include his schooling, early marriage, and fatherhood; the next 25 years as an actor and playwright in London; and the last five in retirement in Stratford where he enjoyed the moderate wealth gained from his theatrical successes. The years linking the first two periods are marked by a lack of information about Shakespeare and are often referred to as the "dark years."

At some point during the "dark years," Shakespeare began his career with a London theatrical company, perhaps in 1589, for he was already an actor and playwright of some note by 1592. Shakespeare apparently wrote and acted for numerous theatrical companies, including Pembroke's Men, and Strange's Men, which later became the Chamberlain's Men, with whom he remained for the rest of his career.

In 1592, the Plague closed the theaters for about two years, and Shakespeare turned to writing book-length narrative poetry. Most notable were "Venus and Adonis" and "The Rape of Lucrece," both of which were dedicated to the Earl of Southampton, whom scholars accept as Shakespeare's friend and benefactor despite a lack of documentation. During this same period, Shakespeare was writing his sonnets, which are more likely signs of the time's fashion rather than actual love poems detailing any particular relationship. He returned to playwriting when theaters reopened in 1594, and did not continue to write poetry. His sonnets were published without his consent in 1609, shortly before his retirement.

Amid all of his success, Shakespeare suffered the loss of his only son, Hamnet, who died in 1596 at the age of 11. But Shakespeare's career continued unabated, and in London in 1599, he became one of the partners in the new Globe Theater, which was built by the Chamberlain's Men.

Shakespeare wrote very little after 1612, which was the year he completed *Henry VIII*. It was during a performance of this play in 1613 that the Globe caught fire and burned to the ground. Sometime between 1610 and 1613, Shakespeare returned to Stratford, where he owned a large house and property, to spend his remaining years with his family.

William Shakespeare died on April 23, 1616, and was buried two days later in the chancel of Holy Trinity Church where he had been baptized exactly 52 years earlier. His literary legacy included 37 plays, 154 sonnets and five major poems.

Incredibly, most of Shakespeare's plays had never been published in anything except pamphlet form and were simply extant as acting scripts stored at the Globe. Theater scripts were not regarded as literary works of art, but only the basis for the performance. Plays were simply a popular form of entertainment for all layers of society in Shakespeare's time. Only the efforts of two of Shakespeare's company, John Heminges and Henry Condell, preserved his 36 plays (minus *Pericles*, the thirty-seventh).

Historical Background

There may not be a play more misnamed in Shakespeare's entire canon than *The Merchant of Venice*. Though he is certainly an important character, Antonio—the merchant in question—merits, at best, fourth billing. The main lovers in the play, Portia and Bassanio, command a great deal more attention, and, as most commentators suggest, Shylock is ultimately the main attraction. Although the Jewish moneylender "appears in only five of the play's twenty scenes, and not at all in the fifth act, everyone agrees that the play belongs to Shylock" (Barnet 193-4). His dominance is such that, in certain productions (particularly in the nineteenth century), the last act has been "omitted entirely" (Myrick, "Introduction" xxii). Yet, despite his somewhat lesser role, Antonio proves crucial to both main plots of *The Merchant of Venice*. His agreement to serve as collateral for Shylock's loan to Bassanio facilitates the latter's courtship of Portia, and the risk to his life which results from this arrangement generates much of the plot's complications. Shakespeare's decision to make him the title character perhaps stems from an acknowledgment of Antonio's structural importance to all the various story lines, as well as from an effort—perhaps unsuccessful—to balance the audience's attention equally between Shylock's thirst for revenge and the romance of Portia and Bassanio.

Antonio's importance as the hinge between the play's two main plots may reflect the fact that Shakespeare had no one particular inspiration for *The Merchant*, but rather drew primarily on two different sources. Both the story of the three caskets and the story of a usurer's demand of a pound of human flesh apparently derive from Oriental folk-tales (Myrick, "Sources" 142-3; Barton 250), though it is likely that Shakespeare encountered them from Italian and Latin sources. A collection of Italian stories, *Il Pecorone*, is usually suggested as Shakespeare's source for the pound of flesh, while *Gesta Romanorum*, a book of medieval Latin stories (first translated into English in 1577), was very likely his introduction to the three caskets (Myrick, "Sources" 142-3). As with most of Shakespeare's plays, the exact date of composition is unknown, but contemporary references prove that it had been performed at least by 1598. "In 1598 and in 1600 the play was entered in the Stationers' Register. It was first published in a quarto (Q1) in 1600" (Myrick, "Textual Note" 139).

The most prominent cultural issues in *The Merchant*, both embodied in the character of Shylock, are the Elizabethan attitudes toward Jews and usury (moneylending). Although "[e]laborate arguments have been mounted to demonstrate that *The Merchant of Venice* is not anti-Semitic"—presumably stemming from critics' desire to defend the ethics of the man many consider to be the greatest poet of the English language—"it is no good to try to discard the hate that energizes the play" (Charney 47). "Jews had been officially banished from England for three centuries" by the time Shakespeare was writing, and there was a lingering hatred of the Jewish race and religion among Christian societies (Barton 250). Such a Christian grudge against Jews allegedly stemmed from the latter group's rejection of Christ, and this sad mixture of racial and religious prejudice is by no means absent from the play. The anti-Semitic mood of England was further fueled by the trial and execution of Roderigo Lopez—a Portuguese Jew and physician to Queen Elizabeth—who was accused of attempting to poison his employer in 1594, a few years before Shakespeare's play was written (Barton 250). The association of Jews with usury is a stereotype unfortunately still familiar to us today; apart from such racial animosity, however, the Elizabethans despised moneylending for interest in and of itself. The practice was technically illegal in England at the time, although there were various ways—some officially-sanctioned—around the law (Myrick, "Introduction" xxvii-iii). The possibility of Antonio's death as a result of his financial dealings with Shylock no doubt reflects the contemporary fear about the exorbitant interest rates usurers sometimes charged.

The stage history of *The Merchant of Venice* has largely been the history of the interpretation of Shylock. How Shakespeare staged the play and the part is unknown; the absence of extensive reference to it throughout the 1600s suggests it wasn't originally one of the author's most popular works (Barnet 194). George Granville staged a notable adaptation of it in 1701, featuring a bumbling, comic Shylock, and this interpretation appears to have been the standard one until 1741, when Charles Macklin radically transformed the character into a terrifying, almost monstrous villain (Barnet 194-6). The next major revision in the acting of the role occurred in 1814, when Edmund Kean presented a Shylock who "evoked not simply terror but pity"; Shylock was seen as justified in his rage, due to his ill-treatment at the hands of the Christians (Barnet 196-7). The evolution of a kinder, gentler Shylock culminated in 1879, when Henry Irving played the character as "a sympathetic and tragic figure," a heroic victim of the increasingly unseemly Christians (Barnet 119). As the dominant Christian culture in England and America has gradually mollified its attitudes toward Jews, Shylock has been portrayed in an increasingly sympathetic light, and subsequent interpretations have oscillated between the various elements of horror and pity, comedy and tragedy, available to the role.

Perhaps the most important aspect of Shakespeare's writing—one which no study guide can presume to replace—is his linguistic style. Indeed, though this may be an obvious point, it is Shakespeare's language (rather than, say, his characters or plots) which has earned him his reputation as the pre-eminent English poet. The large number of expressions or sayings from his plays that have found their way into everyday speech, testifies to the English-speaking world's fascination with Shakespeare as an architect of language. Ironically, however, it is the very strangeness or poetic quality of Shakespeare's language that many beginning students find to be the chief difficulty in coming to terms with his plays, and a few remarks on this subject may serve to clarify some of the peculiarities of Shakespeare's version of English.

It is important to note at the outset that the English of Shakespeare's time and that of our own are relatively the same. That is, both fall under what is broadly designated "Modern English," as opposed to "Old English" (such as one might find in the epic poem *Beowulf*) or "Middle English," (as in Chaucer's *The Canterbury Tales*). Be that as it may, some mitigating factors tend to estrange the present-day reader or audience member from Shakespeare's language. The most obvious of these is age. *The*

Merchant of Venice, for example, is roughly four hundred years old, and while its language may be substantially the same as ours, a great many words, phrases, and even whole syntaxes have altered over the course of time. This can be shown in the following example:

In Act II, scene 1, when the Prince of Morocco attempts to persuade Portia of the value of his dark skin, he remarks, "I tell thee, lady, this aspect of mine/ Hath feared the valiant." There are a number of minor differences easily dispensed with; most English speakers will know "thee" and "hath" are the equivalents of "you" and "has" respectively. The word "aspect" may seem a somewhat unusual or archaic way to refer to "complexion" or "face," but presents no serious difficulty. What is strangest about this sentence is that, for the present-day reader, it seems to say the opposite of what it means. In current usage, to say that someone "feared the valiant" would be to indicate that the person was "afraid of" valiant people. In Shakespeare's time, however, the verb "fear" could also be used to indicate "make afraid" or "cause to fear," a usage which has since died out in our everyday speech. The sense of Morocco's utterance is apparent only in the context of his whole speech, where "afraid of the valiant" wouldn't fit into a list of his complexion's attributes. Such moments may cause a reader confusion in certain passages, but a little detective work usually clears the matter up. A good edition of the play will most likely footnote such passages and explain the disparity.

Not all of the differences between Shakespeare's English and our own are strictly chronological, however. *The Merchant of Venice*, like all of Shakespeare's plays, is written largely in verse, and as such, is estranged from any variety of spoken English. (Although we can make very educated conjectures, we can't, in any case, be positively sure of how English was spoken in Shakespeare's day based on written documents alone. This is, of course, the only evidence available.) Much of what a present-day reader might find estranging in Shakespeare's language is simply due to his poetic techniques. A reader must be prepared to grant Shakespeare a great deal of leeway in his use of language; otherwise the encounter will end in frustration. Sometimes, for example, Shakespeare will concoct a usage of a word different from, but related to, its previous senses. Shylock, in Act II, scene 6, complains of the laziness of his former servant, Launcelot Gobbo, with the remark "Drones hive not with me;/ Therefore I part with him..." A present-day reader is probably not used to seeing "hive" as a verb at all; although it has such uses in Shakespeare's time, he seems to have invented this particular one. According to the Oxford English Dictionary, the earliest recorded usage of "hive" in the sense of "To live together as bees in a hive" is this same example from *The Merchant of Venice* (Compact Edition OED 1312). Shakespeare frequently bends previous senses of his words to accommodate his poetic desires, sometimes initiating new trends in the word's employment.

Shakespeare is at his best (though for the new student most difficult) when he makes words perform tasks they ordinarily don't do, and this is often manifested in more subtle and complicated ways than merely inventing a new-but-related sense for a word. The final example is from the same scene as the previous one and is also spoken by Shylock. In cautioning his daughter Jessica to ignore the Christian revelries taking place on the street below, Shylock says:

> Lock up my doors; and when you hear the drum
> And the vile squealing of the wry-necked fife,
> Clamber not you up to the casements then..."

The phrase in question here is "wry-necked fife," which—strictly speaking—doesn't make sense. A fife is one cylinder-shaped piece; nothing on it could be called its "neck." The phrase might thus be taken to refer to the fife-player, whose neck would be so twisted in order to play the instrument. "Fife" would then be a synecdoche for "fife-player," much as one can refer to a king by saying "the crown." The trouble with this reading is that it doesn't fit with "vile squealing," which would refer to the sound of the fife not the player, and a reader may also be inclined to take "fife" as the instrument in parallel with the reference to "drum." The best solution to this dilemma is to say not that "fife" must refer either to the player or the instrument, but rather that Shakespeare accesses both with his grammatical violation. Both player and instrument are needed to fill out the sense of the sentence, which, though perhaps difficult for new readers, can hardly be construed as a flaw since the poet manages to say two things for the price of one, in a remarkable feat of "verbal economy." Such moments, once the reader is familiar and comfortable enough with the language, become transformed from the poet's greatest difficulty to his chief attraction.

A twentieth-century philosopher, attempting to grasp the significance of and his own difficulty with the most renowned of English poets, once wrote: "I do not believe that Shakespeare can be set along side any other poet. Was he perhaps a *creator of language* rather than a poet?" (Wittgenstein 84). This is perhaps a useful way to conceive of Shakespeare, inasmuch as his plays often create their own rules for language usage and readers must be willing to loosen their hold on their sense of "correct English" in order to partake of them. If anything justifies Shakespeare's reputation as the greatest of English poets, it is such "creative power," the poet's ability to fashion linguistic objects which are not only unprecedented in our language but which subsequently become part of that language.

Master List of Characters

Antonio—*a merchant of Venice and intimate friend of Bassanio.*

Salerio—*friend to both Antonio and Bassanio.*

Solanio—*friend to both Antonio and Bassanio.*

Bassanio—*a young gentleman of Venice in financial difficulty; suitor to Portia and intimate friend of Antonio.*

Lorenzo—*friend of Bassanio and Antonio; Christian lover of the Jewish woman, Jessica.*

Gratiano—*friend of Bassanio and Antonio; joins Bassanio's expedition to Belmont; romancer of Nerissa.*

Portia—*a wealthy heiress of Belmont; she approves of Bassanio's suit to her.*

Nerissa—*Portia's waiting woman and confidante; approves Gratiano's advances.*

Shylock—*a Jewish moneylender of Venice.*

Morocco—*an African Prince and suitor to Portia.*

Launcelot Gobbo—*a clown (comical member of the lower class); ex-servant of Shylock who enters into Bassanio's service.*

Old Gobbo—*Launcelot's father; nearly blind from age.*

Leonardo—*servant of Bassanio.*

Jessica—*daughter of Shylock; Jewish lover of the Christian man, Lorenzo.*

Aragon—*a prince; suitor to Portia.*

Tubal—*a friend of Shylock; a Jew of Venice.*

Jailer—*holds Antonio prisoner.*

Balthasar—*a servant of Portia.*

The Duke of Venice—*the highest authority in Venice.*

Stephano—*a messenger sent by Portia to Lorenzo and Jessica.*

Various Magnificoes of Venice, Officers of the Court, Musicians, Servants, Messengers, *and* **Attendants**

Summary of the Play

Bassanio, a Venetian nobleman with financial difficulties, wishes to compete for the hand of Portia, a wealthy heiress of Belmont, in order to restore his fortune. He asks his friend Antonio, a successful merchant of Venice, to loan him the money necessary to undertake such an attempt. Antonio agrees, but, as all of his assets are tied up at sea, he will have to use his credit in order to obtain the money for his friend. They go to Shylock, a Jewish moneylender and enemy of Antonio's. Shylock agrees to lend them 3000 ducats, but only if Antonio will sign a bond offering the usurer a pound of his flesh if the loan is not repaid in three months' time. Despite Bassanio's misgivings, Antonio assents to the arrangement.

Meanwhile, in Belmont, Portia laments to her serving woman, Nerissa, the terms of her late father's will. They state that whoever seeks to marry Portia must solve the riddle of the three caskets— one gold, one silver, one lead, each with an inscription— or, failing in the attempt, agree to remain a bachelor for the rest of his days. Various suitors attempt the test and fail, until Bassanio arrives. Portia favors him and is delighted when he succeeds. His man, Gratiano, also proposes to Nerissa. She accepts.

But all is not well in Venice. Lorenzo, a friend of Bassanio and Antonio, elopes with Shylock's daughter, Jessica. This enrages Shylock, who vows to show no mercy should Antonio be unable to repay the loan. Much to the usurer's delight, Antonio's ships become lost at sea, placing him in financial jeopardy. Shylock has him arrested and waits eagerly to make good on the bond.

After Bassanio succeeds at the challenge of the caskets, Jessica and Lorenzo arrive in Belmont seeking refuge. Bassanio simultaneously receives a letter from Antonio, revealing his predicament. Having no time to perform the wedding services, Bassanio and Gratiano depart for Venice, promising to return. Leaving Jessica and Lorenzo in charge of her household, Portia, accompanied by Nerissa, secretly leaves for Venice.

In court before the parties concerned, Shylock appeals to the Duke of Venice for the fulfillment of his bond. The Duke is reluctant, but sees no legal way to prevent Shylock's claim. Portia and Nerissa, disguised as a doctor of law and his clerk, arrive to help decide the case. Portia initially rules in favor of Shylock; before he can begin to cut, however, she points out that he is not entitled to spill any of Antonio's blood. She finds him guilty, furthermore, of attempting to take the life of a Venetian citizen. At the mercy of the court, Shylock loses half of his possessions and is forced to convert to Christianity. He leaves in defeat.

In payment for her services, the disguised Portia asks Bassanio for a ring she had given him in Belmont on the condition that he would never part with it. He refuses, and she storms off in pretended anger. Antonio, however, prevails upon his friend to send the ring after the doctor for "his" services to them; Bassanio sends Gratiano, who also gives up the ring Nerissa gave him with the same stipulation, to the clerk.

Portia and Nerissa arrive in Belmont. Pretending they never left, the two woman demand to see the rings they gave their future husbands and feign outrage when they cannot produce them. Portia finally lets everyone off the hook and admits her and Nerissa's roles in the events in Venice. She also gives Antonio a letter informing him that three of his ships have arrived safely in port, restoring his wealth. The group go to Portia's house to celebrate.

Estimated Reading Time

As a rule, students should equip themselves with a well-annotated edition of the play, in order to smooth some of the friction between Elizabethan English and our own variety of the language. One hour per act is a rough guideline for the first read-through. This will vary, of course: Act V, which consists of only one scene, is obviously a great deal shorter than the rest; Acts II and III are longer than average. Certain scenes, such as Act IV, Scene 1, will command more attention than others, given their length and importance. Use your own discretion, and realize that reading Shakespearean English—like encountering any rich and complicated variety of language—becomes easier the more one is exposed to it.

Act I

Act I, Scene 1

New Characters:

Antonio: *a merchant of Venice*

Salerio and Solanio: *friends to Bassanio and Antonio*

Bassanio: *a young gentleman of Venice, friend of Antonio*

Lorenzo: *friend of Bassanio and Antonio, loves Jessica*

Gratiano: *friend of Bassanio and Antonio*

Summary

In Venice, Antonio is depressed, though he is uncertain why. Salerio and Solanio try to account for his sadness by suggesting he is worried about his merchant ships sailing in dangerous waters. Antonio denies this, but can suggest nothing in its place. Salerio and Solanio leave as Bassanio, Lorenzo, and Gratiano enter. Gratiano and Lorenzo jest with Antonio, lifting his spirits slightly, before departing.

Left alone, Bassanio apologizes to Antonio for owing him a great deal of money. Antonio tells him not to worry about it. Bassanio then informs Antonio of a wealthy heiress in Belmont whom he wishes to court. The trouble is, he needs to borrow more money from Antonio to outfit himself properly, in order to compete with the many wealthier suitors. Bassanio suggests that, with a little more money, he will improve his chances of repaying his

debt to his friend. Marrying the heiress will solve all of Bassanio's financial problems. Antonio readily agrees to this plan; however, as all of his capital is tied up at the moment with his ships, he will be unable to lend money directly. Bassanio instead can use Antonio's name to obtain credit.

Analysis

This scene is primarily exposition, conversation made to fill the audience in on the various circumstances leading up to the events of the play. The audience learns about Antonio's generosity and successful business standing, Bassanio's present financial embarrassments, and the prospect of Portia's wealth as the solution to the latter's problems. Crucial financial information about Antonio—which will account for his future predicament—is revealed. His ships are out to sea, tying up his available assets, and this will lead him to seek a loan from Shylock. The news that his ships have been wrecked will make Antonio unable to repay the money.

Act I, Scene 2

New Characters:

Portia: *the wealthy heiress of Belmont*

Nerissa: *her waiting woman*

Summary

In Belmont, Portia confides to Nerissa her distaste for the provisions of her father's will. Portia's father devised a test for anyone seeking her hand in marriage. A would-be suitor must choose among three caskets (ornamental boxes)—one gold, one silver, one lead—one of which contains permission to marry Portia. The suitor must agree, however, that if he makes a wrong choice, he will spend the rest of his days single. This situation is aggravated by Portia's complete distaste for any of her potential husbands. Nerissa names them all, while Portia enumerates her particular dislikes of each. She takes heart in the news that each has announced he will

return home, fearing the strict consequences of her father's test. The two women suddenly remember Bassanio, whom they find more appealing; however, they are interrupted in their praise by a messenger who declares that her suitors seek an audience with her, and that a new contestant, the Prince of Morocco, will arrive soon.

Analysis

This short scene primarily serves as the audience's introduction to the plot of the three caskets, which determines who may marry Portia. The test of the caskets will be performed three times in the play, by Morocco in Act II, Scene 8, Aragon in Act II, Scene 9, and Bassanio in Act III, Scene 2. The audience learns here of Portia's inclination toward Bassanio. Her resentment of her father's will is also significant; Portia is too independent to be told what to do, as becomes clear when, later in the play, she takes matters into her own hands to resolve Antonio's plight. Apart from these important introductions, the substance of the scene is largely comic, a series of jokes based on various prevailing national and ethnic stereotypes as Portia disdains each suitor in turn. As is the case with much of Shakespeare, this scene is an excuse for the playwright to exercise his linguistic ingenuity in constructing clever sentences, such as "When he is best he is a little worse than a man, and when he is worst he is little better than a beast" (lines 86-88).

Act I, Scene 3

New Character:

Shylock: *a Jewish moneylender of Venice*

Summary

In Venice, Bassanio negotiates with Shylock to borrow three thousand ducats (monetary units) for three months, for which "Antonio shall be bound." Shylock doesn't agree immediately, but wishes to speak to Antonio first. Antonio enters, provoking Shylock to vent his hatred of him in an aside. Shylock claims to hate Antonio for being a Christian, for loaning money to people in need without charging interest, and for publicly slandering Shylock's own business practices. Antonio, despite his customary scruples against usury (moneylending for interest), personally asks Shylock to loan Bassanio the money. Still Shylock hesitates, reminding Antonio of the merchant's past ill-treatment of him and suggesting Antonio's hypocrisy in now coming to him for a favor. Antonio is unrepentant, however, claiming that they needn't be friends in order to do business together.

Shylock then turns the tables on his adversaries, suddenly announcing his intention to loan Bassanio the money out of "kindness," i.e., without charging interest. There is one catch, however: Antonio must go with Shylock to a notary and sign an agreement stating that if he fails to repay the loan on time, he must allow Shylock to cut off a pound of his flesh. Shylock claims this is "merry sport," and Antonio readily agrees, treating the whole affair as a gag. Bassanio, however, is alarmed at this arrangement and insists Antonio not enter into the bargain. Antonio is not convinced of any real danger, however, and agrees to meet with Shylock "forthwith" to sign the bond.

Analysis

This is the most complicated scene thus far in the play. Its function is to establish the second major complication of the plot, the bond for a pound of Antonio's flesh. It also introduces the audience to Shylock, possibly the most engaging character in the play. Beyond these plot considerations, however, the ramifications of this scene are immense.

The appearance of Shylock announces two of the play's central issues: the relationship between Jews and Christians, and the Venetian—and by association, the Elizabethan—attitude toward usury. The animosity between Christians and Jews is almost immediately established as the scene unfolds, and, although it is Shylock who first calls these matters to the audience's attention, Antonio confirms that the hostility is mutual. The fact that Shylock is referred to as "the Jew" by the others suggests that their contempt for him is more than merely personal; to them, Shylock represents a group whom they are compelled to dislike for religious and even racial reasons.

It is perhaps impossible for us to decide how much of the animosity between the two Christians and Shylock is personal and how much is based on group identity. Indeed, the characters move between both sets of reasons as if there were no distinction between them, or as if their identities guaranteed the nature of their personal relations. Shylock initiates hostilities in this scene, informing Bassanio that, although he will transact business with him, "I will not eat with you, drink with you, nor pray with you" (lines 34-5). Shylock makes it clear in his speech—with the reference to "pork," a food many Jewish sects forbid its members to consume—that even their culinary differences are religious. His initial expression of disgust for Antonio is explicitly religion-oriented: "I hate him for he is a Christian" (line 39).

Shylock's bitterness, however, next becomes a business matter; Antonio's interest-free loans to the needy "[bring] down/ The rate of usance" in Venice, affecting the usurer's profits. His complaint against Antonio then takes a personal turn, as Shylock recalls, "he rails/ Even there where merchants must do congregate,/ On me, my bargains, and my well-won thrift,/ Which he calls interest" (lines 45-8). The personal tenor of Shylock's hatred is magnified in a later speech, when he confronts Antonio: "You call me misbeliever, cutthroat dog,/ And spet [spit] upon my Jewish gabardine,/ And all for use of that which is mine own" (lines 108-10). Clearly the religious dispute has moved to the level of personal insult, even to mild scuffling. Antonio shows no remorse in the face of such accusations, however, justifying his behavior on moral principles.

The issue of usury seems inextricable from the religious bickering. Antonio equally despises Shylock for his moneylending practices as for his religion and race. It is as if commerce and religion are the same; Antonio's contempt for Shylock's usury may stem from his Christian faith, while for Shylock, there is no contradiction between his profession and his religious convictions. There is, obviously, no one interpretation of this scene which can satisfy all of its possibilities. The Elizabethan distaste for usury no doubt inclined the play's original audience to side with Antonio on this matter. If this is the case, however, we might, along with Shylock, detect a certain hypocrisy in Antonio's coming to him for a loan in a time of need. His principles bend to practical considerations, much like Elizabethan law, which made usury illegal but left provisions that it wouldn't be punished if the interest rate was less than 10%. An audience's feelings about Shylock matter a great deal in this scene, for either he will appear as justifiably resentful of Antonio's seemingly-unprovoked treatment of him, or else as deserving such treatment for his beliefs and practices.

One final aspect of this scene that has been a source of contention among critics concerns the agreement of a pound of flesh as collateral for the loan. Shylock twice refers to the arrangement as "merry," as though the whole affair is in no way a serious one. Some readers of the play have taken him at his word; they believe that he only becomes serious in his demand after Lorenzo, Antonio's friend, runs off with Shylock's daughter Jessica, who in turn steals some of her father's money and possessions. Others argue that the entire arrangement is from start to finish motivated by Shylock's desire for revenge against Antonio.

Study Questions

1. What causes do Salerio and Solanio suggest for Antonio's melancholy?

2. What humorous advice does Gratiano offer Antonio?

3. Why does Bassanio want Antonio to loan him more money?

4. Why is Portia angry with her deceased father?

5. Why does Nerissa tell Portia she "need not fear" her unwelcome suitors?

6. What do Portia and Nerissa think of Bassanio?

7. According to Shylock, why does he hate Antonio?

8. Why is Shylock indignant over Antonio's request?

9. What is Antonio's response to Shylock's accusation?

10. In exchange for what does Shylock agree to lend Antonio and Bassanio the money?

Answers

1. Salerio and Solanio think Antonio is distracted because his money is tied up in his ships, which are sailing on dangerous seas. When he denies this suggestion, Solanio guesses that he's in love, an answer Antonio also rejects.

2. Gratiano tells Antonio not to be so grave about worldly affairs, but rather "With mirth and laughter let old wrinkles come,/…Why should a man whose blood is warm within/ Sit like his grandsire…/…And creep into the jaundice/ By being peevish?" In other words, he suggests Antonio is acting old before his time.

3. Bassanio tells Antonio that "had [he] but the means" to compete with Portia's suitors, he would "questionless be fortunate," i.e., win the wealthy heiress's hand, thus solving his financial difficulties.

4. Because of the provisions of her father's will—the challenge of the three caskets—Portia cannot choose her own husband. As she says, "I may neither choose who I would nor refuse who I dislike, so is the will of a living daughter curbed by the will of a dead father."

5. Nerissa tells Portia she "need not fear" marrying any of the undesirable suitors because "[t]hey have acquainted [Nerissa] with their determinations; which is indeed to return to their home, and trouble [Portia] with no more suit…"

6. Nerissa claims that Bassanio, "of all the men that ever [her] foolish eyes looked upon, was the best deserving a fair lady." Portia agrees and "remember[s] him worthy of [Nerissa's] praise."

7. Shylock claims to hate Antonio because "he is a Christian;/ But more, for in that low simplicity/ He lends out money gratis, and brings down/ The rate of usance here with us in Venice." He also remembers being personally insulted by Antonio.

8. Shylock suggests that Antonio is a hypocrite, having first spurned him for being a usurer and now asking him for a

loan. As Shylock taunts him, "You come to me and you say,/ 'Shylock, we would have moneys'—you say so,/ You that did void your rheum upon my beard…"

9. Antonio insists their mutual hatred is a proper business relationship, telling Shylock, "If thou wilt lend this money, lend it not/ As to thy friends…/ But lend it rather to thine enemy,/ Who if he break, thou mayst with better face/ Exact the penalty."

10. Shylock asks Antonio to sign a bond stating that, if he doesn't repay Shylock within the allotted time, he must sacrifice "an equal pound/ Of [his] fair flesh, to be cut off and taken/ In what part of [his] body pleaseth [Shylock]."

Suggested Essay Topics

1. Compare and contrast Antonio's situation in signing the agreement with Shylock, with Portia's situation of being held bound to her father's will.

2. Contrast Antonio's loans to Bassanio with Shylock's loan to Antonio and Bassanio.

Act II

Act II, Scene 1

New Character:

Morocco: *an African prince, suitor to Portia*

Summary

The Prince of Morocco arrives at Portia's house in Belmont, seeking her hand in marriage. He asks Portia to disregard their racial difference and judge him instead by his personal merits. Portia reminds Morocco that the choice is not hers to make; he, like the other suitors, must face her father's challenge of the three caskets. She assures him, however, that she regards him "as fair/ As any comer [she has] looked on yet/ For [her] affection" (lines 20-22). Morocco laments that, in spite of his valor, mere chance may deprive him of Portia. Portia refers him to the terms of her father's will, which he accepts. They agree to perform the test after dinner.

Analysis

This short scene introduces the audience to the Prince of Morocco, who will make the first unsuccessful attempt to pass the test designed by Portia's father to determine who will marry her. In terms of the play's themes, its chief interest is its explorations of racial animosity, which we have seen earlier in the encounter between Shylock and the two Christians. Morocco requests that Portia "Mislike [him] not for [his] complexion" (line 1) but rather consider him for his personal worth. Although Portia claims that this is her policy, the sincerity of her claim is later called into question at the close of Act II Scene 7. After Morocco fails the test and departs, Portia says in relief "A gentle riddance.../ Let all of his complexion choose me so" (lines 78-9). Unlike Shakespeare's contemporaries, who may have endorsed such sentiments, more modern audiences might perhaps have an ugly impression of the attitudes of the Christians in the play. Though Morocco is a minor character, such scenes may inform the audience's feeling about Shylock and his indictments of Christian hypocrisy.

Act II, Scene 2

New Characters:

Launcelot Gobbo: *ex-servant of Shylock*

Old Gobbo: *Launcelot's father*

Leonardo: *servant of Bassanio*

Summary

This scene opens with Launcelot Gobbo debating whether or not to leave Shylock's service. Just as he decides to quit, his near-blind father, Old Gobbo, arrives with a gift for Shylock. Since his father doesn't recognize him, Launcelot toys with him for a time before revealing his identity. He asks his father to give the gift instead to Bassanio—who subsequently enters with Leonardo—as a means of begging a position in his household. The Gobbos make their pitch and Bassanio accepts, hiring Launcelot on the spot. Bassanio then dispatches Leonardo to prepare his household to receive Antonio for dinner. Gratiano enters and asks Bassanio if he may attend him on his journey to Belmont. Bassanio agrees, but not before cautioning Gratiano to curtail his ribaldry.

Analysis

Little of this scene actually bears much relation to the plot of the play, save the establishment of Gratiano as Bassanio's

attendant. It is more or less an excuse for Shakespeare to indulge his audience with a bit of linguistic comedy, in the form of the Three Stooges-like double-talk spoken by the Gobbos. We should note, however, that even in a scene as light as this one, Shakespeare keeps the issue of racial hostility before his audience. Launcelot's desire to leave Shylock's employ stems largely from the fact that his boss is Jewish, coupled with his belief that the Jew "is a kind of devil" (line 24). Significantly, Shylock is never referred to in this scene by name, but simply as "the Jew."

Act II, Scene 3

New Character:

Jessica: *daughter of Shylock*

Summary

At Shylock's house, Jessica, his daughter, bids farewell to Launcelot as he prepares to leave her father's service. She entreats him to deliver a message to Lorenzo. After he departs, she expresses her desire to marry Lorenzo and become a Christian.

Analysis

This scene sets in motion another important subplot—the romance between Shylock's daughter and Bassanio's and Antonio's friend. Some critics speculate that it is Jessica's departure with Lorenzo, coupled with her theft of her father's money and jewels, that pushes Shylock over the edge and provokes him to pursue the pound of Antonio's flesh in earnest. (Others, of course, claim that this was Shylock's intention all along.) The anti-Semitism of the play is fueled here by Jessica's own self-loathing, i.e., her desire to shed her own religion and become a Christian.

Act II, Scene 4

Summary

Gratiano, Lorenzo, Salerio, and Solanio prepare for an evening of street festivities. Launcelot arrives to deliver Jessica's message to Lorenzo. Lorenzo sends Launcelot back with the reply "I will not fail her," and instructs the messenger to "Speak it privately." Lorenzo explains to Gratiano Jessica's plan to flee her father.

Analysis

This is essentially a development of the subplot begun in Act II, Scene 3, confirming the plan on Lorenzo's end. Lorenzo magnifies the Christians' dislike of "Jew-for-Jews sake" in the following lines: "And never dare misfortune cross [Jessica's] foot,/ Unless she [i.e., misfortune] do it under the excuse,/ That she [Jessica] is issue to a faithless Jew" (lines 35-37). In other words, Lorenzo perceives the "flaw" of Jessica's Jewishness as potentially outweighing her personal merits.

Act II, Scene 5

Summary

Launcelot has come to Shylock's house to deliver the invitation for the usurer to dine with Bassanio and Antonio. Shylock apparently overcomes his earlier religious scruple against dining with the Christians and accepts. He cautions his daughter against the Christian masquers (street-revelers); she is instructed to keep the house shut tight. Before departing, Launcelot secretly informs Jessica that Lorenzo will come by that night. Shylock quizzes his daughter on what just passed between her and Launcelot, but she throws him off the scent. He expresses satisfaction at having Launcelot leave his employ, and then exits to dine at Bassanio's house. Jessica prepares to flee.

Analysis

Like the two preceding scenes and the scene to follow, Act II, Scene 5 sets up the circumstances under which Jessica can rob her father and escape with Lorenzo. This scene perhaps fuels the interpretation that only after Jessica's flight does Shylock become serious in his desire to kill Antonio, as we might well imagine Shylock's feeling duped by the Christians (as though Bassanio lured

him away with the invitation to dinner so Lorenzo and Jessica could elope).

Act II, Scene 6

Summary

Gratiano and Salerio, dressed for the street festivities, stand before Shylock's house, awaiting Lorenzo. As soon as he arrives, Jessica appears "above" (i.e. on the second level of the Elizabethan stage, presumably the second floor of Shylock's residence), disguised as a boy. Lorenzo recognizes her and identifies himself. He asks her to come down and be his torchbearer for the revelry, although she is embarrassed at her present appearance. Lorenzo persuades her to descend; on her way out, Jessica pilfers more ducats from her father. Lorenzo, Jessica, and Salerio depart as Antonio arrives. He detains Gratiano, informing him that the masque is canceled and Bassanio shall sail that evening. This suits Gratiano, and the two men exit to prepare.

Analysis

This scene more or less wraps up the subplot of Jessica's and Lorenzo's elopement, though its consequences—primarily consisting of Shylock's rage—will continue to be felt throughout the play. Jessica and Lorenzo will flee to Belmont, Portia's region, and will mind her household in her absence.

In many of Shakespeare's comedies, there are two separate locales, the court, where normal business occurs according to fairly rigid codes, and a more magical realm where rules are suspended and transformation is possible. In such plays, characters from the first realm visit the second and, on their return to the first, feel renewed. It may be Jessica's and Lorenzo's flight to Belmont and the play's romantic final act which have encouraged some critics to fit The *Merchant of Venice* into this structural pattern. According to such an outline, Venice would be the narrow rule-bound court while Belmont serves as the enchanted land, just like the forest of Arden in *As You Like It* or the woods outside Athens in *A Midsummer Night's Dream*. But this is an over-simplification of

The Merchant, a critical attempt to force it into a pre-ordained pattern rather than attend to the play's particulars. It ignores, for one, the circumstance of Portia's father's will and the challenge of the three caskets. Belmont seems to be as strictly bound by legality and technicality as Venice, and much of the play is devoted to subverting or accommodating the letter of the law in both cities. If anything, *The Merchant of Venice* might foreshadow Shakespeare's later, so-called "problem comedies," such as *Measure for Measure*, in which the levity is tempered by threats of danger. The possibility exists that Portia could end up with an undesirable husband, and the threat to Antonio's life according to the terms of Shylock's bond casts an even darker shadow.

Act II, Scene 7

Summary

Meanwhile, back in Belmont, Morocco prepares to undergo the challenge of the three caskets in order to win Portia's hand, while the lady in question looks on. The prince surveys each casket and its inscription. The first is made of gold and bears the message "Who chooseth me shall gain what many men desire." The second, of silver, reads "Who chooseth me shall get as much as he deserves." The third, finally, is made of lead and warns "Who chooseth me must give and hazard all he hath." Portia informs Morocco that the correct casket contains her picture, signifying success. The prince then deliberates for some time, weighing both factors: the material of each casket and the message on it. By a process of elimination, he chooses the gold one. Much to his chagrin, it contains a death's head and a scroll informing him of his error. Upset, the prince makes a gracious but hasty exit, and Portia expresses her relief at his lack of success.

Analysis

This is the first of three scenes (Act II, Scene 7, Act II, Scene 9, and Act III, Scene 2) displaying the challenge of the three caskets in action. The interest these scenes generate is, in some respects, *not* a dramatic one, for although the fear of an undesirable marriage is a very real one for Portia, it is a great deal less of one for her audience. Indeed, the progressive workings of these scenes are so formulaic that they are almost without any drama at all. Each of the three caskets is successively chosen by each of the three suitors, no choice is repeated, and, of course, the winning casket is the last one picked. By the time Bassanio arrives in Belmont, the audience is well aware of which choice is correct and is simply waiting for him to make it. This contrived inevitability need not be considered a flaw, however; unlike, say, the final scene of a detective drama, where plot and plausibility are of extreme importance, one doesn't read Shakespearean comedy with such demands. The spirit of comedy here suspends issues of realistic plausibility.

The question then becomes, what is the interest these scenes hold for an audience? (Remember, Shakespeare was a successful and popular showman. He wouldn't have dropped *three* such scenes into his play unless they had other, non-dramatic attractions.) The value of these scenes, perhaps, lies in the issues of reading and interpretation which they bring to the foreground. Indeed, the bulk of Act II, Scene 7 (lines 13-60) is devoted to the reasoning process by which Morocco arrives at his choice of the gold casket. What the challenge of the caskets reveals is the flexibility and ambiguity of language, and in this revelation, a reader or theater-goer may find an analogy to his or her own experience of the play. As the need or desire to analyze Shakespeare's plays has already made us aware, certain displays of language require interpretation in order for someone to be able to act on them or even to decide what to think about them. The suitors of Portia engage in a task not terribly different from the audience's own, or from the director's own when he or she decides, for example, how the part of Shylock ought to be acted.

It is important to remember that the choice of the lead casket is only obvious and inevitable in hindsight; Morocco is not to be deemed a fool for his incorrect choice. We might even say that, of all of Portia's suitors, the Prince is the one most unfairly duped by the process of casket selection. His interpretation of the inscription "Who chooseth me shall gain what many men desire" as signifying Portia is a sound one, for as he points out, "All the world desires her;/ From the four corners of the earth they come/ To kiss

this shrine, this mortal breathing saint" (lines 38-40). The courting of Portia is central to *The Merchant of Venice*; it sets the entire plot in motion, as Bassanio's need of additional capital to outfit himself is the reason Antonio becomes indebted to Shylock in the first place. Perpetual chastity—the penalty for choosing the wrong casket—is a highly improbable interpretation of "what many men desire." It is, indeed, the opposite of desire. Whereas it is relatively easy to imagine the silver casket's inscription as the wrong choice (i.e., the man in question may not "deserve" Portia and may rather deserve the punishment for his presumptuousness), an audience may very well feel that Morocco has been lied to.

The underhandedness with which Morocco is treated might be, however, in keeping with the racial hostilities permeating the play. As Shylock is automatically excluded by the others for his Jewishness, the Prince is disliked, among other reasons perhaps, for his skin color. Morocco's first utterance in the play (line 1) is a plea for racial tolerance; he is on the defensive at the outset. Although Portia assures him in Act II, Scene 1 that his race is not a factor in her acceptance—and we must assume this is true, insofar as, by the rules of her father's will, Portia must marry whoever makes the right choice—her tolerance is called into question at the end of this scene. After Morocco departs, Portia breathes a sigh of relief and says "Let all of his complexion choose me so" (line 79), continuing the theme in the play that one is automatically included or excluded from the circle of favorable people in Christian society according to one's religion or race. Portia can't even imagine meeting a black man who could satisfy her and dismisses "all" of them in one sentence.

Act II, Scene 8

Summary

This scene consists entirely of a brief conversation between Salerio and Solanio, aimed at informing the audience of a variety of events which have occurred while the scene in Belmont was taking place. The audience learns that Shylock has discovered his deception, that his daughter has run off with his money and

Lorenzo. Shylock is white with rage, much to the amusement of Christian Venice. Salerio reveals that Bassanio's ship is underway for Belmont. He also reports the news that a Venetian vessel has been wrecked in the English Channel, and worries that it might be Antonio's. Solanio recalls witnessing Bassanio's departure, and Antonio's melancholy at their separation. Salerio and Solanio resolve to seek Antonio out to attempt to cheer him.

Analysis

This is another scene of pure exposition, providing the audience with information crucial to advancing various strains of the plot as they currently stand. Some critics have made much of Shylock's confused lamentation concerning his daughter and his ducats, ascribing various aspects to his character based upon his equating of the two. One ought to keep in mind, however, that this is a reported speech; the audience doesn't witness Shylock making such a spectacle, which mitigates the speech's effect on the audience.

Other critics have suggested the possibility of a homosexual relationship between Bassanio and Antonio, or at least a strong homosexual attachment to his friend on Antonio's part. It could be argued that Antonio's general sadness throughout the play stems from the prospect of his intimate friend turning away from their love by entering a heterosexual partnership with Portia. While the evidence of a sexual friendship between Bassanio and Antonio is too scant to insist on, it is clear that the latter's attachment for the former extends beyond the bounds of simple friendship. Not only does Antonio loan Bassanio money with only a shaky prospect of repayment, but he freely and willingly risks his life for his friend's happiness. Clearly Bassanio is Antonio's primary attachment, which makes it no surprise that, in a play that ends with three marriages, Antonio remains conspicuously single.

Act II, Scene 9

New Character:

Aragon: *a prince, suitor to Portia*

Summary

The Prince of Aragon undertakes the challenge of the caskets to win Portia's hand, agreeing to abide by the rules of her father's will. He dismisses the lead casket immediately, not thinking it worth the "hazard." He next considers the golden chest, reading its inscription of "what many men desire" as implying a lack of discrimination. Finally, he selects the silver, believing he must "deserve" that which he seeks. Much to his dismay, however, the silver casket contains a fool's head and a scroll informing him of his error. Aragon leaves. A messenger then arrives, informing Portia that a Venetian lord is on his way to try to win her. Nerissa hopes aloud that it is Bassanio.

Analysis

This is the second of the three casket selecting scenes. Aragon is a bolder, less-subtle reasoner than Morocco and makes his incorrect choice quickly, firm in his belief of his own merit. Yet for that, his justification for choosing the silver casket is an eloquent one and may arouse an audience's admiration. The casket's own interpretation of what its selector "deserves" (i.e. the presumptuous man is a fool and deserves to be treated to a fool's head) is, however, a more justifiable one than that of the gold casket.

Study Questions

1. Why does Morocco fear Portia will reject him at the outset?

2. What is Bassanio's reservation about Gratiano accompanying him to Belmont?

3. What is Jessica's dilemma concerning her father, Shylock?

4. How does Lorenzo plan to disguise Jessica in order for her to escape from her father?

5. Before going to dine with Antonio and Bassanio, what advice does Shylock give his daughter?

6. Why does Jessica not want Lorenzo to see her when he arrives at Shylock's house?

7. What is Morocco's rationale for choosing the gold casket?

8. What news has Salerio heard, making him anxious?

9. How does Solanio interpret Antonio's sadness at Bassanio's departure?

10. Which casket does Aragon choose, and why?

Answers

1. Morocco fears Portia would not want to marry someone of his race. Upon entering the play, he pleads: "Mislike not for my complexion/ The shadowed livery of the burnished sun..."

2. Bassanio suspects that Gratiano will appear "too wild, too rude, and bold of voice" for the people of Belmont. "[W]here thou art not known," Bassanio warns, such traits "show/ Something too liberal."

3. Jessica believes it is a "heinous sin.../ To be ashamed to be [her] father's child!" Although she is Shylock's daughter by "blood," she claims not to be by "manners" and hopes to become a Christian by marrying Lorenzo.

4. Jessica will be dressed as Lorenzo's torchbearer for the street festivities.

5. Shylock tells Jessica that if she hears commotion outside, she should "Clamber not...up to the casements then,/ Nor thrust [her] head into the public street/ To gaze on Christian fools.../ But.../ [she should] Let not the sound of shallow fopp'ry enter/ [his] sober house."

6. Jessica is ashamed because she has been "transformed to a boy," i.e. is dressed in men's clothing in order to make her escape.

7. The gold casket is engraved "Who chooseth me shall gain what many men desire." As Morocco points out, "All the world desires [Portia];/ From the four corners of the earth they come/ To kiss this shrine, this mortal breathing saint."

8. A Frenchman informed him that a Venetian ship has been wrecked in the English Channel, and Salerio fears it may be one of Antonio's.

9. Solanio believes that Antonio "only loves the world for [Bassanio]." In other words, his friendship with Bassanio is the one thing which keeps Antonio from being overwhelmed by melancholy.

10. Aragon selects the silver casket, engraved "Who chooseth me shall get as much as he deserves," because, he asks, "who shall go about/ To cozen fortune, and be honorable/ Without the stamp of merit? Let none presume/ To wear an undeserved dignity." Aragon feels whoever wins Portia had better be deserving of her.

Suggested Essay Topics

1. What is the relationship—both structurally and thematically—of the Jessica/Lorenzo subplot to the main plots of The *Merchant of Venice*?

2. Compare and contrast Morocco's reasoning during the selection of caskets with Aragon's speech during the same test.

3. Aside from the obvious one of comic relief, what function might Launcelot Gobbo be seen to have in the play?

Act III

Act III, Scene 1

New Character:

Tubal: *a Jewish friend of Shylock*

Summary

In Venice, Salerio and Solanio discuss Antonio's financial state. Salerio has received confirmation that one of Antonio's merchant vessels was wrecked in the English channel. As the two lament this ill news, Shylock enters. He is bitter with both men for their knowledge of Jessica's elopement before the fact, but they simply mock him in return. The conversation turns to Antonio, on whom Shylock is intent on wreaking his revenge according to the terms of the bond. Salerio asks Shylock what good a pound of Antonio's flesh will do him, but Shylock dismisses this line of questioning as irrelevant. He is after vengeance, not reimbursement.

Salerio and Solanio learn from a messenger that Antonio awaits them at his house. As they leave, a friend of Shylock's, Tubal, arrives with news concerning both Jessica and Antonio. In Genoa, Tubal learned that another of Antonio's ships was lost coming away from Tripoli. Shylock rejoices at the news, but this is soon tempered by the knowledge that Jessica has been frivolously spending his money. He is dismayed to find that she has traded (for a monkey) a ring given him by his wife, but Tubal comforts him by reminding him of Antonio's bad luck. Shylock asks Tubal to arrange

to have an officer arrest Antonio, and they part, making plans to meet later at their synagogue.

Analysis

The plot thickens for Antonio, threatening to make him a pound thinner. Not one, but two, of his ships, the audience learns, have come to ruin, throwing his finances into chaos and bankruptcy. Shylock already feels he has grounds to detain the merchant, in order to insure his adherence to the terms of their bond. The next time Antonio appears on stage (Act III, Scene 3), he will be in the custody of a jailer.

As is the case in most scenes in which he appears, however, Shylock steals the show here. He utters one of the most famous speeches of the play, if not of Shakespeare generally, the "Hath not a Jew eyes?" monologue (lines 55-69). This speech may initially strike a reader or audience member as an eloquent plea for racial and religious harmony, climaxing in the dramatic lines, "If you prick us, do we not bleed? If you tickle us, do we not laugh? If you poison us, do we not die?" (lines 61-63). There is, however, a sinister undercurrent running throughout the speech; Shylock follows the above lines with "And if you wrong us, shall we not revenge?" (line 63). In this line, the plea for harmony explicitly spills over into the harsher "eye-for-an-eye" sentiments of Mosaic Law. Keep in mind that the tension in this speech is between its forceful eloquence and its purpose as a justification for performing brutal violence against Antonio. The skilled talkers in Shakespeare's plays—be they as silly as Polonius in *Hamlet* or as repulsive as Caliban in *The Tempest*—always command an audience's attention and consideration. One must acknowledge a certain righteousness in Shylock's position. He has been abused at the hands of the Christians before, and now he has just cause to suspect Antonio's complicity in his daughter's flight.

One interesting detail which perhaps does more than any other to humanize Shylock and enlist audience sympathy is his grief over the loss of a ring given him by his wife (whose absence from Shylock's household throughout the play may indicate that he is a widower). Shylock's outrage over his daughter's theft moves from the economic to the personal, as he wouldn't have parted with this item for any price. The audience may be more perplexed than ever at the end of this scene, as both Shylock's venom and his humanity increase.

Act III, Scene 2

Summary

Act III, Scene 2 contains the first major climactic moment in the play, as one of its two main plots—Bassanio's quest for Portia and the challenge of the three caskets—comes to a resolution. The scene opens with Bassanio and his attendants at Portia's house in Belmont. For the first time in Th*e Merchant of Venice*, Portia exhibits enthusiasm for her potential suitor. She bids Bassanio to delay his choice, so that, in the event of his failure, they will still have had a chance to spend time together. Bassanio refuses, however, impatient to get the trial over with. Portia makes a speech praising him and wishing him success. A song is sung while Bassanio deliberates in silence.

After the song, Bassanio reasons aloud over the caskets. Unlike his predecessors, Bassanio primarily concentrates on the material of the caskets rather than the descriptions. Distrusting the lure of appearance, he chooses the leaden one, which contains a picture of Portia and a congratulatory note. Bassanio kisses Portia, according to the instructions. Portia proclaims her unworthiness, before giving herself and all of her possessions over to Bassanio. She offers him a ring, with the proviso that if he take it from his finger or lose it, he indicates the end of his love for her. Bassanio swears to keep the ring, till death do them part.

In the mirth which ensues, Gratiano suddenly reveals that he and Nerissa are to be wed and receives permission to do so at Bassanio's and Portia's wedding. At that moment, Salerio arrives from Venice, accompanied by the fugitives, Jessica and Lorenzo. Salerio delivers a letter from Antonio to Bassanio. As Bassanio reads, Portia observes that he loses his gaiety, and she demands to know the message. Bassanio reveals to her his indebtedness to Antonio and the fact that all of the latter's ventures at sea have failed. Salerio informs his friends of Shylock's absolute refusal to

settle for anything less than the terms of his bond (i.e., the pound of Antonio's flesh).

Perceiving the closeness between her future husband and his friend, Portia offers to pay the debt to Shylock twelve times over. All she requests is that Bassanio marry her before setting out. When she discovers that Antonio's life is at stake and that he begs to see Bassanio one last time before dying, however, Portia dispatches Bassanio immediately. He promises to return as soon as possible.

Analysis

Act III, Scene 2 is one of the longest and most important scenes in the entire play. Its primary purpose is to show how Bassanio solves the riddle of the caskets and win Portia. Beyond that, it sets up or continues the other storylines which will lead to the resolution of the pound of flesh plot.

The first item of significance in the scene is the fact of Portia's enthusiasm for Bassanio's attempt to win her hand. This is unprecedented in the play and, true to the spirit of comedy, Portia obtains her choice even though the terms of her father's will allow her no choice.

The next major aspect of the scene is Bassanio's solution to the challenge of the caskets. He announces his logic at the very beginning of his attempt: "So may the outward shows be least themselves;/ The world is still deceived with ornament" (lines 73-4). In other words, he knows the lure of the surface may be misleading and refuses to be taken in by mere appearances. Interestingly, Bassanio eschews the inscriptions of the caskets entirely and this, the audience might feel, is wise. Already we have seen how the same words can be bent to virtually opposite ends. Although it could be argued that the legend on the gold casket is misleading, the silver and lead caskets' inscriptions could easily be read as invitations or as warnings. This is not to say that Bassanio avoids linguistic matters entirely; far from it. He instead balances his distrust of appearances against the cultural significance of all three metals. By his rationale, the least worthy casket by outward appearances—lead, a metal of no cultural worth—becomes the correct choice. And so it is.

Bassanio's future marriage to Portia guarantees him financial security and the wherewithal to pay his debts to Antonio. This, we might recall, was ostensibly his motive for seeking Portia's hand in the first place, though it appears that he and Portia, at this point in the play, are genuinely in love. Paying off Antonio becomes a largely irrelevant concern, in any case. Portia seems to have more money than she knows what to do with; Antonio discharges his friend from his debts as long as Bassanio returns to Venice before his execution; Shylock will never collect on his 3,000 ducat loan in skin or cash. After all these complications, the audience may feel, Bassanio and Portia had better be in love!

As one plot is resolved, another more minor plot is introduced in the form of the ring Portia gives Bassanio to seal their love. Portia ends up generating the remaining portion of the play beyond Act IV, Scene 1 with her mischievous shenanigans involving the ring. Otherwise the play would end after Act IV, Scene 1, once the pound of flesh plot is concluded. The reason for this extra plot perhaps stems from a desire on Shakespeare's part to thicken the mix of his play with some pure comedy. Though the threat against Antonio's life ends happily, it may have been deemed too grim a scenario to end the comedy on.

Act III, Scene 3

New Character:

The Jailer: holds Antonio on Shylock's behalf

Summary

Meanwhile, back in Venice, Shylock encounters Antonio on the streets, albeit in the custody of the Jailer hired to guard him and accompanied by Solanio. Antonio begs a word with the usurer, but Shylock won't even listen to him. "I'll have no speaking; I will have my bond" (line 17) he cries before departing. Solanio tries to encourage Antonio, saying the Duke will not permit the fulfilling of the bond, but Antonio is resigned to his death. He knows it is important to law and order (as well as the economy) in Venice that the Duke uphold Shylock's legal right to have his bond fulfilled.

Antonio seems to have reconciled himself to his impending doom, so long as Bassanio returns to Venice to see him one last time.

Analysis

For the most part, this scene serves to put us back in touch with Venice after the previous long scene in Belmont, to assure the audience that things are indeed going as badly as Bassanio and company think they are. Aside from this, it advances the image of an unyielding, bitter Shylock and a melancholy, resigned merchant of Venice. Antonio's last lines are interesting, however: "Pray God Bassanio come/ To see me pay his debt, and then I care not!" (lines 35-6). After his magnanimous, even passionate displays towards Bassanio, these lines ring with an almost spiteful bitterness. Perhaps there is some sexual jealousy on Antonio's part, the way he recalls Bassanio from his future bride's side in order to tell him, "I would die for you."

Act III, Scene 4

New Character:

Balthasar: *a servant of Portia*

Summary

Portia begins this scene in discussion with Lorenzo, during which she commits the management of her household to his and Jessica's hands. She informs him that she and Nerissa are going to a monastery to pray until her husband comes home. After Jessica and Lorenzo exit, however, Portia instructs her servant Balthasar to deliver a letter to her cousin Dr. Bellario (a lawyer) and bring whatever clothes and instructions he offers to the ferry, where she will be waiting. He goes, and Portia informs Nerissa that they are to travel to Venice disguised as men, for purposes she will explain shortly.

Analysis

From this point in the play onward, Portia takes a central and commanding role. It's as if, freed from the strictures of her father's will after Bassanio's triumph, Portia now seeks to make up for lost time by solving Antonio's dilemma. Not only is she convinced of Antonio's worth on the basis of his friendship with Bassanio (as she informs Lorenzo), but also, one might speculate, she feels indebted to him for enabling his friend's trip to Belmont.

Portia acknowledges the fact that being a woman has kept her sidelined from the action thus far, in a speech which the Elizabethan audience probably would have found humorous, but which more liberal-minded audiences today would no doubt receive with more sympathy. The play is fraught with images of women's servitude, and their problematic positions as second-class citizens. Clearly, Portia is submissive to her father even after his death, and her wealth and power are transferred to her husband immediately following her marriage. It is important to note that these constraints are placed upon and accepted by the most powerful woman in the play. In even more subtle terms, as the couples pair off in Act III, Scene 2, they wager about who will be the first to have a male child, underscoring the desirability of males over females to the Elizabethans. In an exercise of what little power she has, Portia camps it up with some swagger at the expense of the men in her society, poking fun at their self-aggrandizing bluster and making bawdy references to their anatomy. What Portia and Nerissa are about to do, as the audience will learn shortly (in Act IV, Scene 1), is disguise themselves as a lawyer and his clerk, in order to arbitrate the bond between Antonio and Shylock, in another subtle way showing that in order to move in the Venetian circles of power, they must disguise their gender.

Act III, Scene 5

Summary

Launcelot teases Jessica about her genealogy, claiming that being a Jew, she is damned. On the subject of genealogy, Lorenzo walks in and announces that Launcelot has gotten "the Moor" (i.e., a black woman) pregnant. Launcelot and Lorenzo match wits good-naturedly for a time, before the former departs. Lorenzo and Jessica flirt for a few lines before departing for dinner.

Analysis

This is a gratuitous scene, thrown in solely for laughs rather than plot. It does, however, flirt comically with two of the play's themes. Jessica's Jewish ancestry is mocked here, although in a purely light-hearted way. It seems that suddenly, no one takes Jessica's ethnicity seriously anymore, which is quite a reversal from previous scenes. Keep in mind that, even for Lorenzo—who is in love with Jessica—the issue of her race at one point threatened to outweigh any of her particular behavioral characteristics.

Also invoked here is the trouble with words, which previously had manifested itself in relation to the challenge of the three caskets. Lorenzo, exasperated with the linguistic displays of Launcelot, laments "How every fool can play upon the word!" (line 43). Lorenzo's plea to Launcelot—"I pray thee understand a plain man in his plain meaning" (line 57)—is a humorous and perhaps nostalgic wish for language to be fixed in its meaning and not available to multiple interpretations.

Study Questions

1. Why, since it won't result in any financial gain, does Shylock insist on the terms of his bond with Antonio?

2. What news does Tubal bring Shylock?

3. Why does Portia want Bassanio to wait before facing the challenge of the three caskets?

4. Why does Bassanio select the lead casket?

5. What does the lead casket contain?

6. What does Portia claim will occur if Bassanio gives up the ring she gives him?

7. What does Gratiano reveal after Bassanio solves the riddle of the three caskets?

8. Why does Portia allow Bassanio to leave before they get married?

9. According to Antonio, why won't the Duke be able to intercede on his behalf?

10.   What does Portia decide to do at the end of Act III?

Answers

1.   Shylock wishes to cut off Antonio's flesh in order to "feed [his] revenge. [Antonio] hath disgraced [him]…laughed at [his] losses…scorned [his] nation, [and] thwarted [his] bargains" out of (so Shylock claims) pure racial hostility.

2.   Tubal tells Shylock that one of Antonio's ships has been wrecked "coming from Tripolis" and that Jessica has spent a great deal of his money.

3.   Afraid that Bassanio will fail, but desirous of his company, Portia wishes to spend as much time with him as possible.

4.   Bassanio distrusts attractive surfaces, for fear they contain corrupt things. As he addresses his choice, "But thou, thou meager lead/ Which rather threaten'st than dost promise ought,/ Thy paleness moves me more to eloquence;/ And here choose I."

5.   Inside the lead casket, Bassanio finds a picture of Portia—signifying his success—and a scroll instructing him to kiss her.

6.   If Bassanio does "part from, lose, or give away [Portia's ring],/ …it [will] presage the ruins of [his] love."

7.   Gratiano announces that he and Nerissa intend to marry.

8.   Portia discovers, while reading Antonio's letter, that he fears "it is impossible [he] should live" and wishes to see Bassanio before he is killed.

9.   "The Duke cannot deny the course of the law;/ For the commodity that strangers have/ …in Venice, if it be denied,/ Will much impede the justice of the state." In other words, the Duke must uphold the law for non-citizens, so that Venice may maintain its good standing in international business affairs.

10.   Portia decides that she and Nerissa must go to Venice disguised as men, to help resolve the situation there.

Suggested Essay Topics

1. Compare and contrast Bassanio's deliberations over the three caskets with those of his rivals.

2. Discuss Shylock's "Hath not a Jew eyes?" speech in relation to the various attitudes toward race demonstrated throughout the play.

3. How does Portia's character develop over the course of Act III?

Act IV

Act IV, Scene 1

New Character:

The Duke of Venice: *highest authority in Venice*

Summary

Bassanio and his attendants are back in Venice and wait with Antonio in the presence of the Duke to discover the fate of the merchant of Venice. Shylock enters the court, and the Duke makes a personal appeal to him to not only spare Antonio's life but also, in light of the merchant's recent losses at sea, to reduce the amount of the debt. But Shylock will have none of it, demanding that the bond be executed. When questioned on his motives, Shylock responds that he simply hates Antonio and is not obliged to have any particular justification. Bassanio offers Shylock twice the amount of Antonio's debt, but the latter remains firm. Shylock reminds the Duke that it is necessary to uphold the law in order to maintain Venice's good standing in international trade.

The Duke declares that he will make no decision until he hears from Bellario of Padua, who he has asked to come decide the matter. Nerissa enters, dressed in men's clothes, posing as a messenger from Bellario. She gives the Duke a letter, which he reads while Gratiano and Shylock bicker. The Duke reveals that the letter recommends a young doctor (lawyer) to the Venetians to help decide the case. The Duke sends for the man while the letter is read to the court.

This "man" is actually Portia, disguised as a lawyer. She questions Shylock and Antonio on the particularities of their case, and asks Shylock if he would be merciful. He refuses, of course. Bassanio, offering to pay the debt twice over, asks the disguised Portia if they might bend the law in this particular case. Much to Shylock's delight, however, she declares this cannot be, for it would set a dangerous legal precedent in Venetian law. Portia asks Shylock if he'll take three times the amount of the debt and spare Antonio's life, but he refuses to budge. She decrees that the bond must be adhered to. Antonio thus steels himself for death.

Before Shylock can start slicing away, however, Portia points out that although he is perfectly entitled to Antonio's flesh, he has no claim to spill any of the merchant's blood. Moreover, should he do so, his "land and goods/ Are by the laws of Venice confiscate/ Unto the state of Venice" (ll. 309-311). Shylock is dismayed by this news and seeing no way to obtain Antonio's flesh without bloodshed, asks for the money instead. Portia prevents Bassanio from handing over the money, however, insisting that justice must be served. She points out, however, that Shylock will be subject to execution if he takes more or less than a pound of flesh.

Realizing that his sinister jig is up, Shylock attempts to slink away with only the original 3,000 ducats. Portia won't allow this, however, as he has already "refused it in open court." Shylock sees he is trapped and is prepared to leave court empty-handed. But Portia produces another law, decreeing that if any foreigner "by direct or indirect attempts/ …seek[s] the life of a citizen," he loses half his goods to the citizen, the other half to the state, and his "life lies in the mercy/ Of the Duke…" The Christians take great delight in this, and the Duke spares Shylock's life though confiscates his wealth.

Embittered, Shylock asks that he be killed, as he cannot sustain himself without his goods. Antonio intercedes, however, and asks the Duke to pardon the state's portion of the fine, in exchange for the following conditions: Antonio must receive half of Shylock's goods to use in trust for Lorenzo and Jessica; Shylock must become a Christian; and he must will all his possessions upon his death to Jessica and Lorenzo. The Duke agrees to this arrangement, as does Shylock, who has little choice. Shylock then pleads illness and hobbles away from the scene a broken man.

The Duke requests that Portia dine with him, but she begs off, claiming she must return to Padua. The Duke leaves. Bassanio and Antonio offer to pay the disguised Portia the 3,000 ducats earmarked for Shylock, but she refuses, claiming satisfaction in justice. Bassanio presses, so Portia asks for his gloves, which he gives her, and his ring, which he holds back. He pleads first the ring's worthlessness, and then his sentimental attachment to it. Portia scorns him in pretended outrage, and she and Nerissa depart. Antonio then persuades Bassanio to let the lawyer have the ring, for the service "he" rendered. Bassanio relents and sends Gratiano with his ring to find the pair.

Analysis

This scene marks the resolution of the second major plot complication of *The Merchant of Venice*, namely the pound of flesh scenario. There doesn't seem much point in denying that the play climaxes with this particular scene, and that the remaining scenes constitute little more than some good-natured dénouement. It is also the last scene of which Shylock is part, and so central is he deemed to the play that several productions have ended here, omitting the rest altogether. This is perhaps appropriate, for with Shylock go all the issues which have been preoccupying the audience for the length of the play. The sole remaining concern is the subplot of the rings, which was only introduced into the plot in the preceding scene and is quite extraneous to the major business on stage.

Shylock enters the scene well past the point of reconciliation; he wants Antonio dead, and will accept no amount of money in exchange for foregoing the terms of his bond. The issue of Jewishness comes to a head at this point, as the Christians attribute Shylock's stubbornness to an inbred racial/religious sensibility. Antonio even asks his friends not to try to change Shylock's mind, for, he feels, "You may as well forbid the mountain pines/ To wag their high tops and to make no noise/ When they are fretten with the gusts of heaven;/ You may as well do any thing most hard/ As seek to soften.../ His Jewish heart" (lines 75-80). Shylock's rigidity is seen to stem from his constitution. The usurer himself, however, belies this claim, for, we may recall from Act III, Scene 1, Shylock insists he learned this behavior from "Christian example."

The Christian animosity towards Shylock's Jewishness is made most apparent, however, in the terms of Shylock's punishment. The most conspicuous of Antonio's three conditions for Shylock is the demand that he must convert to Christianity. Some stage productions of The Merchant have given a great deal of weight to this detail, representing it as the crushing blow to the usurer. This is a convincing interpretation, insofar as Shylock appears to take his religion very seriously throughout the play. Moreover, shortly after the demand has been made and agreed to, Shylock must leave the court, pleading illness. It's as if the idea of conversion is physically repugnant to him. Given his treatment at the hands of the Christians, it may very well be.

An issue somewhat related to these religious matters is the traditional opposition between the letter and the spirit of the law. Some critics have suggested that the dispute between the Christians and Shylock boils down to the latter's stubborn insistence on formally codified laws as opposed to the spirit in which such laws were written. They further insist that this trait is in keeping with the Elizabethan conception of Jews as cold-hearted exploiters of legal language, a sensibility expressed today in the stereotypes of the lawyer as a shrewd manipulator of language against truth and justice, and as typically Jewish. This binary opposition between Jew/letter and Christian/spirit seems forced, however, when held against the background of Act IV, Scene 1. The Christians, especially Portia, are brutally clever manipulators of the law, as evinced through their juxtaposing of various laws to transform Shylock from a violated creditor waiting to receive his due, to an impoverished supplicant of the Duke, suing for mercy. Portia proves particularly adept at pulling laws out of her assumed hat of "Doctor." It is difficult to say how convincing an audience might find her reasoning that the bond doesn't entitle Shylock to spill any of Antonio's blood; one could argue that the bond doesn't exclude it either, or that the idea of spilling blood is presumed in the idea of cutting off a pound of flesh. (The bond doesn't specifically entitle Shylock to hold the knife with his hand, but it would be difficult to imagine arguing on such grounds.) In any case, it seems petty to fault Shylock for adhering to the letter of the law because, as a Jew in a Christian society, what else does he have to protect him? The "spirit" in Venice is not very friendly to him. The Christians clearly don't want Shylock to have his way and continue to maneuver until they succeed at circumventing his legal claims, however brutal.

The theme of Antonio's possible homosexual love for Bassanio perhaps attains its loudest crescendo here. The morbidity and melancholy which Antonio has from time to time exhibited throughout the play reaches new depths, as throughout the scene he demonstrates a peculiar willingness to die. This eagerness might be accounted for if, as Solanio insists in Act II, Scene 8, Antonio "only loves the world" for Bassanio's presence. Perhaps Antonio feels he has already lost his friend to the world of heterosexual love and would just as soon be killed by Shylock as not. As Antonio steels himself for slaughter, he tells Bassanio, "Commend me to your honorable wife./ Tell her the process of Antonio's end,/ Say how I loved you, speak me fair in death;/ and when the tale is told, bid her be judge/ Whether Bassanio had not once a love" (lines 272-6). An actor could deliver these lines with a great deal of spite, as if to suggest Bassanio had a love and, upon Antonio's death, would no longer have one. In other words, Antonio suggests, no heterosexual relationship could supplant, replace, or even compare with the love he and Bassanio shared.

The last item one might note about Act IV, Scene 1 is the continuance of the subplot of Portia's ring. Upon Shylock's quitting the court, there's no particular reason for Portia and Nerissa to maintain their secret identities. But rather than reveal themselves, the women instead embark upon some gratuitous tomfoolery at the expense of their future husbands. Portia creates the new conflict out of thin air. It's as if, freed from her father's will and armed with a new sense of subjective agency, Portia is reluctant to relinquish her new-found power. Perhaps she is sowing her wild oats, given that, according to the custom of the time, all of Portia's property and possessions will become Bassanio's upon their marriage, and he will be her lord and master. Rather than go directly from one guardian to another, Portia wishes to prolong her freedom and express herself through her own action. This is offset, however, by the fact that her action remains hidden by her disguise, and at its boldest, remains all in fun; she offers no challenge to this social order, especially in light of the fact that her actions are, in the end,

a service to her husband.

It should be noted, finally, that Bassanio initially passes Portia's test of his devotion by refusing to part with the ring. But rather than reveal herself then, she storms off in pretended anger, giving Bassanio time to cave in. Portia is determined to have her fun, it seems.

Act IV, Scene 2

Summary

Gratiano overtakes Portia and Nerissa as they seek Shylock's house in order to have the usurer sign the deed willing his properties to Lorenzo. Gratiano offers Portia the ring and an invitation to dinner. She accepts the former and declines the latter. Nerissa, meanwhile, determines to lure Gratiano into the same trap Portia laid for Bassanio, and sets off with Gratiano, ostensibly in search of Shylock's house, in order to obtain her future husband's ring.

Analysis

This scene simply serves to advance the ring plot by giving Portia the chance to obtain Bassanio's ring and allowing Nerissa the same opportunity with Gratiano, in order to complete the comic symmetry.

Study Questions

1. What does the Duke request of Shylock?

2. What reason does Shylock give for his wanting the pound of Antonio's flesh?

3. Why does Antonio advise his friends to give up attempting to dissuade Shylock?

4. Why does Shylock believe the Duke must enforce the terms of the bond?

5. Why does Portia, disguised as the lawyer, initially conclude that Shylock's bond must be adhered to?

6. Although she acknowledges Shylock's right to a pound of

Antonio's flesh, how does Portia prevent the usurer from acting on it?

7. Why is Shylock stripped of his possessions?

8. Apart from the financial conditions, what does Antonio's new arrangement demand of Shylock?

9. What does the disguised Portia demand from Bassanio for her services?

10. Why is Bassanio reluctant to give up the ring?

Answers

1. The Duke asks Shylock if he will "not only loose the forfeiture,/ But touched with human gentleness and love,/ Forgive a moiety of the principle,/ Glancing an eye of pity on [Antonio's] losses." In other words, he asks Shylock to consider Antonio's financial predicament and not only accept money in place of the pound of flesh, but also reduce the amount of the debt.

2. Shylock claims he can "give no reason, nor will [he] not,/ More than a lodged hate and a certain loathing/ [He] bear[s] Antonio…"

3. Antonio believes that Shylock cannot be reasoned with, due to a racially-determined stubbornness within him. He claims, "You may as well do any thing most hard/ As seek to soften that—than which what's harder?—/ His Jewish heart."

4. Shylock thinks that the Duke must uphold the terms of the bond, otherwise all Venetian law will be held up to scorn and ridicule.

5. Portia insists that there is "no power in Venice/ Can alter a device established," i.e., Shylock's bond can't be changed after its terms have already been violated.

6. Portia points out that, although it allows Shylock to cut away a pound of Antonio's flesh, "This bond doth give [Shylock] here no jot of blood…"

7. Shylock's goods are confiscated because Venetian law decrees such a penalty to a foreigner who "by direct or

indirect attempts...seek[s] the life of any citizen..."

8. Shylock must convert from Judaism to Christianity.

9. Portia asks for Bassanio's gloves and his ring.

10. Bassanio promised Portia that he'd take it off only when he'd stopped loving her.

Suggested Essay Topics

1. What factors motivate Antonio's resignation in Act IV, Scene 1? Discuss this in relation to his ambiguous position of both envying his friend's new relationship and yet sacrificing himself to make it possible.

2. How does the plot of the rings relate to the other contractual obligations dramatized in the play?

3. Consider and discuss the process by which Portia turns the situation in the court from Shylock's advantage to Antonio's.

Act V

Act V, Scene 1

New Character:

Stephano: *a messenger*

Summary

Lorenzo and Jessica are in the garden in front of Portia's house in Belmont, whispering sweet nothings in each other's ears. Stephano, a messenger, enters and announces that Portia will soon return. Launcelot Gobbo arrives and makes the same announcement with respect to Bassanio. Lorenzo dispatches Stephano to ready the household for Portia's return. Lorenzo babbles for a time about the moon and music.

Portia and Nerissa enter and encounter the two mooning lovers, who welcome them home. Portia orders that no one in her household mention her and Nerissa's absence. Bassanio, Antonio, Gratiano, and their followers arrive. Portia welcomes them home to Belmont and is introduced to Antonio.

The company notice Gratiano and Nerissa quarreling. Portia inquires why, and it is revealed that Gratiano gave away the ring Nerissa had given him, which he promised never to remove from his hand. Portia chastises Gratiano, claiming that her betrothed, Bassanio, would never do such a thing. Gratiano reveals that Bassanio too gave his ring away and pleads that they both sacrificed their rings to the judge and clerk, who would take no other

payment. Portia and Nerissa feign disbelief, insisting the men must have given the rings away during some tawdry sexual encounter and vowing never to sleep with their future husbands until the rings are recovered.

Antonio attempts to intercede on his friends' behalf, promising that never again will Bassanio break his oath. To seal the bargain, Portia produces a ring, which turns out to be the same as the one she gave him in the first place. She claims to have recovered it by sleeping with the doctor. Nerissa also insists that she regained her ring from the clerk using a similar method. Having thoroughly bewildered all parties concerned, Portia reveals that she and Nerissa were the doctor and the clerk. She also gives Antonio a letter, informing him that three of his ships have in fact returned and are laden with riches. Nerissa tells Lorenzo of Shylock's new will, naming him heir of the usurer's estate. There is general merriment, and the company goes inside Portia's house.

Analysis

Act V, Scene 1 is the final scene of the play, and its primary purpose seems to be to restore the comic mood threatened by Shylock's attempt on Antonio's life. The frivolous final subplot is resolved here; Portia reveals that she and Nerissa were the doctor and the clerk, and thus that Bassanio and Gratiano simply gave the rings back to their original owners. Clearing away any remaining ill residue from the previous scenes, Portia also reveals that some of Antonio's ships have returned safe, thus restoring his previous good fortune as a businessman. The spirit of comedy wins the day.

Shakespeare's primary agenda in this scene, as in so many, is a linguistic one; in other words, much of the dialogue here is aimed at displaying his wit and ingenuity, with a barrage of puns, double-entendres, and metaphors. Lorenzo's sole purpose in this scene, for example, is to make long decorous speeches, which advance nothing in the play, save its poetry. In particular, Shakespeare milks the humorous potential in Portia's and Nerissa's secret activities for as many double meanings as possible. Nerissa's accusation, that "The clerk will ne'er wear hair on's face that had [the ring from

Gratiano]," for example, has two main senses, one for most of the characters—i.e., Nerissa claims to suspect Gratiano of giving his ring not to a clerk but to another woman—and an extra one for Nerissa, Portia, and the audience—i.e., the clerk, who was actually Nerissa, therefore a woman, will indeed never grow a beard. The chief interest and delight in this scene, one might argue, is the sight of Bassanio and Gratiano squirming, while Portia and Nerissa rattle off string after string of accusations which the women know are both false and true, depending on how one interprets the words. This ties the last scene into the recurring theme of multiple interpretations of words which runs throughout the play. The difference here is that unlike the scenes involving the three caskets, in which much was at stake depending on how one reads the words in question, the final scene offers us this linguistic play for its own sake—just for laughs, as it were—in a spirit of comedy where several interpretations are available and no one—audience and cast alike—is obliged to settle on a single reading to the exclusion of all others. And such is perhaps the ultimate attraction of Shakespearean comedy.

Study Questions

1. What message does Stephano deliver to Lorenzo and Jessica?

2. What opinion does Lorenzo hold of men who don't like music?

3. What does Portia order her household not to do?

4. To whom does Nerissa claim to believe Gratiano gave his ring?

5. What does Portia threaten when Bassanio admits he gave the ring away?

6. What does Portia claim she will do if she encounters the doctor to whom Bassanio gave the ring?

7. How does Antonio attempt to placate Portia?

8. What does Portia offer Bassanio to seal the new promise?

9. What secret does Portia reveal to the company?

10. What good news does Portia tell Antonio?

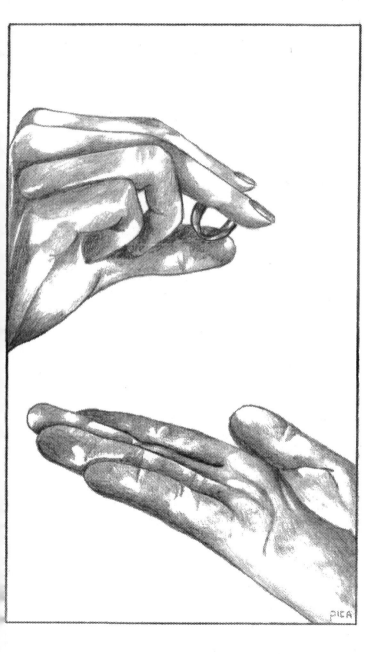

Answers

1. Stephano announces that Portia "will before the break of day/ Be here at Belmont. She doth stray about/ By holy crosses where she kneels and prays/ For happy wedlock hours."

2. Lorenzo claims that "The man that hath no music in himself,/ Nor is not moved with concord of sweet sounds,/ Is fit for treasons, stratagems, and spoils" and is thus not to be trusted.

3. Portia insists that no one reveal that she and Nerissa have been away from home.

4. Nerissa claims whoever has the ring "will ne'er wear hair on's face…" In other words, she says she suspects him of giving it to a woman.

5. Portia swears that she "will ne'er come in [Bassanio's] bed/ Until [she] see[s] the ring!"

6. Portia says to Bassanio, "Since [the Doctor] hath got the jewel that I loved,/ And that which you did swear to keep for me,/ I will become as liberal as you,/ I'll not deny him anything I have,/ No, not my body nor my husband's bed."

7. Antonio promises Portia that "[his] soul upon the forfeit… [Bassanio]/ Will never more break faith advisedly."

8. Portia offers the same ring she initially gave Bassanio, claiming she recovered it by sleeping with the doctor.

9. Portia reveals that she and Nerissa were in fact the doctor and his clerk.

10. Portia gives Antonio a letter in which it is revealed that "three of [his] argosies [i.e., ships]/ Are richly come to harbor suddenly."

Suggested Essay Topics

1. Trace the development of Portia from a daughter bound by her father's will to a behind-the-scenes manipulator of events.

2. How do Lorenzo's speeches concerning the moon and music suggest other themes previously explored in *The Merchant of Venice?*

3. What purpose does the parallel romance of Gratiano and Nerissa serve in terms of an audience's evaluation of the relationship between Bassanio and Portia?

Sample Analytical Paper Topics

The following paper topics are based on the entire play. Following each topic is a thesis and a sample outline. Use these as a starting point for your paper.

Topic #1

Much of the plot of *The Merchant of Venice* is generated by contractual obligations. These take the form of legally binding contracts, such as the bond between Antonio and Shylock, as well as less formal arrangements, such as the ring given by Portia to Bassanio. Examine the way the individual will is forced to negotiate with external demands.

Outline

I. Thesis Statement: *One of the major conflicts illustrated in* The Merchant of Venice *is the struggle of the individual will against the imposed obligations of society. This struggle is primarily manifested through the various contracts characters must fulfill throughout the course of the play.*

II. Act I

    A. Bassanio owes Antonio money and seeks to repay his debt by marrying Portia, a wealthy heiress.

    B. Portia must marry whoever can solve the riddle of the three caskets, as specified in her late father's will.

C.   Many of Portia's suitors give up their attempt to win her hand, unwilling to abide by the strict consequences of her father's will.

D.   Antonio, in the past, has helped people escape the consequences of their contracts with Shylock, the usurer, by lending them money at no interest.

E.   Antonio must sign a bond promising to sacrifice a pound of his flesh to Shylock, so that the usurer will lend Bassanio money for his quest.

III.   Act II

A.   Morocco objects to the terms of Portia's father's will, because it doesn't allow the individual to succeed on his own merits.

B.   Gratiano must agree to curb his usual behavior if Bassanio is to allow him to join his expedition.

C.   Morocco must leave Portia and remain a bachelor for the rest of his life, for failing to solve the riddle of the three caskets.

D.   Aragon suffers the same fate as Morocco for failing in his choice.

IV.   Act III

A.   Shylock intends to have Antonio arrested for being unable to repay the loan on time.

B.   Portia desires Bassanio to wait before attempting to solve the riddle, knowing that, if he fails, she won't be permitted to see him.

C.   Bassanio wins Portia by fulfilling the terms of her father's will.

D.   Portia gives Bassanio a ring which he must wear to prove his love for her.

E.   Gratiano, whose proposal was contingent on Bassanio's success, becomes engaged to Nerissa.

F. Antonio's life is in danger as he has failed to repay his debt to Shylock on time.

G. Antonio absolves Bassanio of all debt, on the condition that the latter comes to Venice immediately, before the merchant's death.

H. Antonio has been taken into custody so that he cannot escape from Shylock.

V. Act IV

A. The Duke feels he cannot stop Shylock's quest for Antonio's flesh without breaking the law.

B. Shylock insists the Venetians must allow him to fulfill the terms of his bond, otherwise Venice will lose its good international standing.

C. Portia, disguised as a doctor of law, informs Bassanio that "There is no power in Venice/ Can alter a decree established."

D. Portia informs Shylock that, although entitled to a pound of Antonio's flesh, he has no legal right to spill any of the merchant's blood.

E. Portia decrees that, according to Venetian law, Shylock is liable to a fine and possible execution for attempting to harm a citizen.

F. Shylock is forced to sign a deed, willing his possessions upon his death to Lorenzo and agreeing to become a Christian.

G. Portia, disguised as the lawyer, demands Bassanio's ring in payment for her services, but Bassanio must refuse, due to his prior agreement with Portia.

H. Bassanio breaks his agreement with Portia by giving the disguised Portia her ring.

I. Gratiano breaks a parallel agreement with Nerissa.

VI. Act V

    A. Portia and Nerissa censure their future husbands for violating their agreements about the rings.

    B. Portia reveals that she and Nerissa provoked the violation.

Topic #2

Much is made of differences between races and religions in *The Merchant of Venice.* Explore the various, sometimes inconsistent attitudes toward, and behaviors based upon, these aspects of culture as they are exhibited in Shakespeare's play.

Outline

I. Thesis Statement: *In* The Merchant of Venice, *characters display an impulse to categorize one another on the basis of religious and racial characteristics, but this is frequently complicated by certain characters' actual behavior.*

II. Act I

    A. Portia and Nerissa discuss the former's suitors on the basis of their national/racial characteristics.

    B. Shylock refuses to dine with Bassanio and Antonio for religious reasons.

    C. Shylock tells the audience that he hates Antonio "for he is a Christian..."

    D. Antonio, in the past, has publicly scorned Shylock for both his religion and occupation.

    E. Antonio thinks that Shylock has overcome some of his Jewish characteristics when he lends the merchant the 3,000 ducats.

III. Act II

    A. Morocco, on meeting Portia, asks her to "Mislike [him] not for [his] complexion" (i.e. to not hold their racial differences against him).

B. Portia assures Morocco that his race cannot be a factor in her decision to wed.

C. Launcelot Gobbo decides to terminate his employment with Shylock because Shylock is a Jew.

D. Launcelot believes Jessica may yet marry a Christian, despite being Jewish.

E. Jessica regrets her Jewish blood and hopes Lorenzo will make a Christian out of her.

F. Lorenzo worries that Jessica's personal merits might not prove sufficient to offset her Jewishness.

G. Shylock decides to dine with the Christians, despite their religious differences.

H. Shylock expresses contempt for the Christians' street festivities.

I. When Morocco departs after failing to solve the riddle of the caskets, Jessica expresses relief that she will not have to marry one of his "complexion."

J. Shylock, it is reported, is outraged that his daughter has fled with a Christian.

IV. Act III

A. Salerio claims that there is a vast difference between Shylock and his daughter, despite their blood relationship.

B. Shylock makes an impassioned speech denying an inherent difference between Christians and Jews, though also claiming that his desire for revenge is not inborn malice but rather behavior learned from Christians.

C. Launcelot teases Jessica that she is damned for being a Jew.

V. Act IV

A. Antonio claims it is pointless to reason with Shylock because he is a Jew.

B. Shylock points out that the Venetians keep slaves who are not allowed to mix with Christian society.

C. Portia, disguised as the young judge, informs Shylock that he is not allowed to spill "Christian blood."

D. The Duke attributes his own mercy toward Shylock to "the difference of our (i.e., the Christians') spirit."

E. Shylock is forced to become a Christian as punishment for his deeds.

Topic #3

In *The Merchant of Venice,* a great deal of emphasis is placed upon the interpretation of ambiguous phrases. Contrast the light-hearted play with ambiguity as embodied in the character of Launcelot Gobbo with either the more purposeful and consequential scenes of the three caskets or the trial scene pitting Portia against Shylock.

Outline

I. Thesis statement: *Shakespeare presents two types of ambiguity in* The Merchant of Venice, *one which the audience is invited to enjoy for its comic merits, the other which the audience recognizes to have serious—perhaps even deadly—consequences. This can be illustrated by contrasting the scenes involving Launcelot Gobbo with those concerning _____.*

II. Launcelot Gobbo.

A. Launcelot often mispronounces or mis-selects his words, lending them an inappropriate or even opposite sense to what he intends to convey.

B. Launcelot evades responsibility for his impregnating "the Moor," by transforming her—through a series of verbal twists and turns—into a linguistic display, involving puns on "much," "more," "less," and "Moor" (Act III, Scene 5).

C. Launcelot manages to shirk his minor household duties by reinterpreting the commands into senses inappropriate to the particular context.

III. The Riddle of the Three Caskets.

    A. Whoever correctly interprets the inscriptions in order to solve the riddle of the three caskets wins Portia's hand.

    B. Whoever fails to interpret correctly the inscriptions in order to solve the riddle of the three caskets must leave Portia and also may never marry anyone else.

    C. Morocco is tricked into choosing the wrong casket by a very improbable interpretation of the inscription on the gold casket.

    D. Aragon misinterprets the inscription on the silver casket through his own conceit.

    E. Bassanio correctly interprets the riddle by concentrating not on the slippery language of the inscriptions but rather on the materials from which the caskets are constructed.

IV. The Trial Scene to Decide Antonio's Fate.

    A. Shylock insists on a strict, unambiguous interpretation of the law, in order to allow him to claim the pound of flesh Antonio has signed over to him.

    B. Neither Bassanio nor the Duke can think of an interpretation of the law or Shylock's bond which would allow for Antonio's escape.

    C. Portia, disguised as the doctor of law, insists that the bond must be adhered to and that Shylock is entitled to a pound of Antonio's flesh.

    D. Shylock insists that nowhere in the bond does it specify that he must declare his motives, or demonstrate mercy, or provide a surgeon to prevent Antonio from dying from his wounds.

    E. Portia reinterprets Shylock's bond by widening its context. In other words, she brings up factors not accounted for in the words of the bond, and rules that Shylock is not allowed to spill blood because the bond doesn't provide for it. There is, of course, no way for Shylock to cut Antonio without making him bleed.

F. Portia invokes other laws in conjunction with the case at hand, to demonstrate that Shylock has broken the law and is subject to financial penalties and possibly death.

G. The Christians draft a new deed, dictating Shylock's future behavior.

Topic #4

Various characters in *The Merchant of Venice* undergo transformations during the course of the play, but none more dramatically or substantially than Portia. Discuss Portia's transformation from her role as the submissive daughter at the beginning of the play to her position as manipulator of events by the end.

Outline

I. Thesis Statement: *The character of Portia may be seen as one who moves from a submissive to a domineering role over the course of events in* The Merchant of Venice. *In doing so, Portia sheds the role traditionally allotted to women in her society and assume a position of power usually reserved for men. This is best exemplified in the trial scene, in which Portia literally assumes a male position in her disguise as a young doctor of law.*

II. Act I

A. Portia is bitter over the terms of her father's will, which stipulates that whoever solves the riddle of the three caskets wins her hand in marriage, leaving her no choice in the matter of her husband.

B. None of Portia's present suitors appeals to her, but she must let them attempt to solve the riddle.

III. Act II

A. Portia informs Morocco that "In terms of choice [she is] not solely led/ By nice direction of a maiden's eyes./ Besides, the lott'ry of [her] destiny/ Bars her the right of voluntary choosing."

B. Portia expresses great relief when Morocco fails to solve the riddle of the three caskets, as she didn't want to marry

him but would have been unable to refuse had he suc-
ceeded.

C. Portia tells Aragon that "If [he] choose[s] that [casket] wherein [she is] contained,/ Straight shall [their] nuptial rites be solemnized."

D. Portia refers to herself as "worthless," due to her inability to control her destiny.

IV. Act III

A. Portia begs Bassanio to wait before attempting to solve the riddle, telling him: "I would detain you here some month or two/ Before you venture for me. I could teach you/ How to choose right, but then I am foresworn./ So will I never be. So may you miss me." She expresses frustration as she finally has a suitor she esteems but cannot marry if he should fail to solve the riddle.

B. Portia is freed from the tyranny of her father's will when Bassanio makes the correct choice.

C. According to the custom of her day, Portia "commits [herself] to [Bassanio's will] to be directed,/ As from her lord, her governor, her king."

D. Portia offers to pay off Antonio's debt, in order to relieve his plight at the hands of Shylock.

E. Portia decides to disguise herself and Nerissa as men—a doctor of law and his clerk—in order to prevent Antonio from losing a pound of his flesh at the hands of Shylock.

V. Act IV

A. Portia is introduced to the Venetian court as Balthazar, "a young doctor of Rome," and is enlisted by the Duke of Venice to help settle the dispute between Antonio and Shylock.

B. Portia questions Antonio and Shylock on the particulars of the case, supporting her judgments in reference to Venetian law.

C.   Using her knowledge of Venetian law, Portia turns the tables on Shylock, so that he is at the mercy of the court and Antonio is freed from the threat of death.

D.   Portia, still disguised, tricks Bassanio into giving her the ring that he earlier promised her he'd never part with.

VI. Act V

A.   Portia arrives in Belmont ahead of Bassanio and informs her household not to reveal her absence.

B.   Portia grills Bassanio over his loss of the ring, declaring they cannot be together faithfully unless the ring is restored.

C.   Portia brings the play to a happy conclusion. She reveals her role in the trial of Antonio, letting Bassanio off the hook for giving up her ring, and she informs Antonio that some of his ships have arrived safely, restoring to him much of his lost fortune.

Bibliography

Barnet, Sylvan. "*The Merchant of Venice* on the Stage." Shakespeare 192-205.

Barton, Anne. "Introduction to *The Merchant of Venice*." *The Riverside Shakespeare*. By William Shakespeare. Eds. G. Blakemore Evans, et al. Boston: Houghton Mifflin Co., 1974. 250-253.

Charney, Maurice. *All of Shakespeare*. New York: Columbia University Press, 1993.

Compact Edition of the Oxford English Dictionary, The Oxford: Oxford University Press, 1971.

Myrick, Kenneth. Introduction. Shakespeare xxi-xxxviii.

—. "Textual Note." Shakespeare 139-141.

—. "A Note on the Sources of *The Merchant of Venice*." Shakespeare 142-144.

Shakespeare, William. *The Merchant of Venice*. Ed. Kenneth Myrick. Rev. ed. New York: Signet Classic, 1987.

Wittgenstein, Ludwig. *Culture And Value*. Eds. G.H. Von Wright and Heikki Nyman. Trans. Peter Winch. Chicago: University of Chicago Press, 1980.

REA's

HANDBOOK OF

ENGLISH

Grammar, Style, and Writing

All the essentials that you need are contained in this simple and practical book

Learn quickly and easily all you need to know about

- Rules and exceptions in grammar
- Spelling and proper punctuation
- Common errors in sentence structure
- Correct usage from 2,000 examples
- Effective writing skills

Complete practice exercises with answers follow each chapter

R\E\A RESEARCH & EDUCATION ASSOCIATION

ilable at your local bookstore or order directly from us by sending in coupon below.

THE BEST TEST PREPARATION FOR THE

AP ADVANCED PLACEMENT EXAMINATION

ENGLISH
Literature & Composition

by Pauline Beard, Ph.D. • Robert Liftig, Ed.D. • James Malek, Ph.D. •
James Maloney, M.A. • Joanne Miller, M.A. • Peter Trenouth, M.A. • Mattie Williams, M.A.

6 Full-Length Exams

➤ Every question based on the current exams
➤ The ONLY test preparation book with detailed explanations to every question
➤ Far more comprehensive than any other test preparation book

Includes a COMPREHENSIVE AP COURSE REVIEW,
emphasizing all areas of literature & composition found on the exam

REA *Research & Education Association*

Available at your local bookstore or order directly from us by sending in coupon bel

806104